# Pursue Your Purpose, Not Your Dreams

# Facilitator's Guide

*Written in collaboration with Progressive Bridges, Inc., 2015*

# *Pursue Your Purpose, Not Your Dreams*
# Table of Contents

| Lesson Title | Guide | Student Text | Portfolio |
|---|---|---|---|
| **Vocabulary Practice** | p. | NA | p. 7 |
| **Lesson 1: Introduction** | p. | Intro. | p. 9 |
| **Lesson 2: Purpose vs. Dreams** | p. | 1 | p. 13 |
| **Lesson 3: What is your Cool?** | p. | 2 | p. 17 |
| **Lesson 4: The Negative Things in Your Life!** | p. | 3 | p. 21 |
| **Lesson 5: Positive Thinking** | p. | 4 | p. 26 |
| **Lesson 6: Facing the Realities of Life** | p. | 5 | p. 30 |
| **Lesson 7: Check Yourself** | p. | 6 | p. 34 |
| **Lesson 8: Rebuilding You** | p. | 7 | p. 38 |
| **Lesson 9: The ISM's of Life** | p. | 8 | p. 42 |
| **Lesson 10: Building Your Team** | p. | 9 | p. 46 |
| **Lesson 11: Don't Get it Twisted** | p. | 10 | p. 50 |
| **Lesson 12: Wrap-Up** | p. | | p. 54 |
| *Pursue Your Purpose* **Checklist** | p. | | p. 59 |
| *Pursue Your Purpose* **Rubric** | p. | | p. 60 |
| **Pre/Post Test** | p. | | NA |
| **Pre/Post Test Answer Key** | p. | | NA |
| **College & Career Readiness Checklist** | p. | | NA |

# *Pursue Your Purpose, Not Your Dreams*
# Facilitator Guide

**Introduction:**

The Facilitator's Guide is supportive in guiding facilitators in utilizing *Pursue Your Purpose, Not Your Dreams* with college students to its fullest benefit. The Facilitator Guide is comprised of 12 student lessons, a roommate/parent connection component, assessments, and a College & Career Checklist, all focused on success in the classroom and life. The lesson menus are flexible enough to be used in 30-90 minute sessions or over a week's time depending upon the number of activities completed. This guide pulls together specific content for the user to empower higher education institutions and other groups working with this population on a new level.

**Student Lessons:**

**Overview of Lesson Components**

Specific areas of literacy: Utilizing Informational Text, Writing, Speaking, and Listening. Many lesson activities utilize College and Career Readiness Skills, noted with a 🎓, and align with the American School Counselor Association Standards as noted toward the back of the Facilitator Guide. Student lessons are organized in a "before, during, and after format" for simple use and contain activities in the following specific areas:

Speaking & Listening

Informational Reading

Research & Writing

It is important before every lesson to preview it in its entirety well in advance. This allows time for lesson customization for specific audiences.

### Before the Lesson

"Before the lesson" focuses on building student readiness prior to introduction of the lesson content. Every lesson begins with a **Lesson Focus** to ensure primary lesson points. Specific lesson vocabulary is introduced in the **Wise Words** section prior to the lesson content, providing students with some background knowledge of essential concepts included in the lesson. Page 7 contains a vocabulary activities menu to support facilitators in teaching new vocabulary found in each chapter. Students have this same menu in their My Purpose Pathway Portfolio so that they can work independently on the vocabulary right in their portfolios.

### During the Lesson

"During the lesson" highlights the lesson content delivered through reading the student book, as well as a **Discuss It** menu of thought-provoking questions and speaking and listening activities designed to engage college students with the lesson content.

### After the Lesson

"After the lesson" focuses on student interaction, application, and personalization with the lesson content. The **Activities Menus** are divided into specific areas: **Inscribe It!** (comprehending content and writing), **Action!** (application of content), **Pursue Possibilities** (extending content), and **Log It!** (personal goal setting). Activities are designed for student to student interaction as they engage in knowledge application, self-analysis, and problem-solving together.

### Roommate and or Parent/Guardian Connection Activities

A menu of **Pursue Your Purpose Home Connection Activities** encourage parent interaction at home as part of every lesson. This menu is a page designed for homework and knowledge extension. All activities encourage student- roommate and or parent/guardian interaction and/or student-community interaction of some kind.

**Assessments:**

**Pre and Post Assessment**

A **Pre and Post Assessment**, a simple method of measuring growth of student knowledge throughout the program, is included in the Facilitator Guide. These assessments can be copied for student use as appropriate before and after the program has been implemented.

**Application-Based Assessments**

The *Pursue Your Purpose* **Checklist** can be made available for daily use as a self-assessment and/or professor/instructor assessment throughout the program. Students can view at a glance the *Pursue Your Purpose* behaviors that are needed for success. Having students complete the checklist builds self-awareness, self-esteem, and growth.

The *Pursue Your Purpose* **Rubric** is available for daily use by students with persistent behavior challenges. Both students and professors/instructors can rate the exhibition of proactive *Pursue Your Purpose* behaviors and measure over time the increase in positive behaviors evident during the semester or academic school year. The rubric lends itself well to graphing progress and measuring the presence of the behaviors listed on the Pursue Your Purpose Checklist. It is suggested the two pages are copied front and back to reinforce these behavior with consistent use.

***My Purpose Pathway* Portfolio**

The ***My Purpose Pathway* Portfolio** kept throughout the lessons promotes student engagement with the *Pursue Your Purpose* text and documents student growth in knowledge and understanding through self-reflection, written responses to positive quotes, research-related project planning, personal journal entries, personal goal setting, and more! Self-reflection is one of the key principles to social-emotional growth. The student portfolio allows for a consumable personal response to the text and the activities done in class that are more interactive in nature.

# *Pursue Your Purpose, Not Your Dreams*

## Best Practices in Teaching Vocabulary

**Word Sorts:** Organize all of the vocabulary words into groupings that have common characteristics. Make up as many grouping titles as needed to go with the groupings.

**Word Map:** Draw a map of the following information all hooked to the center (the vocabulary word): synonyms, antonyms, definition, part of speech, other word forms, used in a sentence from the text, used in your own sentence, visual sketch.

**Symbolize It:** Choose 5 wise words from your chapter list. Construct a picture, graphic, or symbol for each word that captures to meaning of the word.

**SCUBA Diving with Vocabulary:**

   a. S – **Sound** it out. Say the whole word to yourself a couple of times.
   b. C – **Check** the clues in the sentence and paragraph and think about what word would fit best in place of the unknown word.
   c. U – **Use** the text's main idea to make a good guess for the word's meaning.
   d. B – **Break** the word into parts that have meanings that you recognize, and/or think of similar words.
   e. A – **Ask** for help from a peer or teacher, or use the internet.

**Wise Word Debate:** Use at least 5 words meaningfully in a written debate supporting your position about any current topic in today's news. Be sure your debate or argument makes sense.

# Wise Words

| Lesson 1 | Lesson 2 | Lesson 3 | Lesson 4 |
|---|---|---|---|
| Dreamed | Distinctions | Professional | Pessimist |
| Gravitated | Destined | Influence | Barrier |
| Stressed | Jeopardized | Internally | Hurdle |
| Counseling | Burnout | Coolness | Obstacle |
| Reflections | Gratification | Befriend | Impediment |
| Focus | Regrets | Portrayal | Courage |
| Academically | Misinterpretation | Perceptions | Tenacity |
| Devastating | Devastating | Evaluate | Repel |
| Transformation | Pursue | Re-Define | |
| Networking | | Motivational | |

| Lesson 5 | Lesson 6 | Lesson 7 | Lesson 8 |
|---|---|---|---|
| Unforseen | Acknowledge | Maximizing | Rebuilding |
| Capability | Potential | Potential | Dismantle |
| Commitment | Reputation | Recognize | Transitioning |
| Dysfunctional | Pressure | Unfulfilled | Reassemble |
| Internal | Considered | Destruction | Exposing |
| Paralyze | Dimensional | Reputation | Academically |
| Rational | Satisfaction | Distinct | Committing |
| Perceived | Anxious | Perspective | Potential |
| Fortunate | Conquering | Identity | Engaged |
| Jeopardized | Distress | Situational | Attempted |

| Lesson 9 | Lesson 10 | Lesson 11 | Lesson 12 |
|---|---|---|---|
| Heterosexism | Inherited | Translate | Possibility |
| Interactions | Mastered | Possibilities | Issues |
| Ableism | Sacrificing | Conditioned | Overshadows |
| Capacities | Franchise | Acceptance | Maturity |
| Sexism | Encouragement | Phrases | Purposefully |
| Superiority | Presence | Journey | Guidance |
| Covert | Progressing | Pressure | Mental |
| Overt | Aligned | Interpretation | Concerned |
| Racism | Mindful | Role | Circumstances |
| Microaggressions | Accountable | Passion | Syndrome |
| Classism | | | |

# *Pursue Your Purpose, Not Your Dreams*

**Lesson 1      INTRODUCTION**

**Lesson Focus:** This lesson will have students apply their understanding to the introduction and purpose of this book.

**Wise Words:**

| | |
|---|---|
| Dreamed | Gravitated |
| Stressed | Counseling |
| Reflections | Focus |
| Academically | Devastating |
| Transformation | Networking |

**Wise Words Practice:** Choose an activity from the menu on page 7 to introduce words to students in class. Independent student vocabulary practice activities can also be found in corresponding Pathway Portfolio chapter.

**Discuss It:**

⚑ In the beginning of this text, Joe Johnson explains a few words in his introduction that motivated his writing of this book. He uses the words proud and pride. What do these two words mean to you? Define them in your own terms? Share with a partner and compare and contrast your own definitions.

⚑ In the forward, Joe Johnson includes why he is writing this book and who it is for. He wants to encourage and inspire individuals to work on issues of self-esteem, self-doubt and lack of skill development. What do you think motivated him to help people? Have you ever felt motivated to share an experience to help someone? Explain and share your thoughts with a partner.

## Inscribe It: (Reflection Journals)

✝ Look at the content page on page "v" of the book. Review what is inside this book. Make an inference on what you will be reading about in this book. What are the titles of the chapters? How do you think this is going to help you in life? Write your thoughts down in paragraph form and share your thoughts with the class.

✝ On page 1 there is a quote that begins the introduction. Reread this quote several times to yourself. What does this mean to you? How is this a positive application to life? Think about this quote and write down your thoughts. Share with a partner or the class.

## Action!:

✝ At the beginning of Joe Johnson's introduction he tells his story and purpose of writing this book. Create a timeline listing the events he explains. You can complete this on a sheet of paper or poster=sized paper.

✝ Everyone has different life events and shares different emotions that lead them in different directions in life. Read through Joe Johnson's introduction and story of writing this book. Think about how you can relate to what he is saying. What is it? Is there anything in your life that you can relate to from his story? Create a graphic organizer comparing and contrasting your story to Joe Johnson's

✝ Reflecting on your life is a major part of this introduction to this book. Have you reflected on your life? Create a one page movie or magazine cover that exhibits a reflection of your life. You can use drawings or printouts to visually show examples. Make sure to write a small biography about yourself on the cover. *If you have never written a bio, please research online for examples.*

## Pursue Possibilities:

⚐ Research what reflection of one's life means. Create a slide show of what you found. In your general research did you come across anything different that you didn't expect? Present your research using a presentation software or Poster Board.

⚐ Create a slideshow of your life using pictures, music, videos, old letters, etc. Present your slideshow using a presentation software or Poster Board.

⚐ Find a magazine or news article that explains dreams. In this article be sure to identify what made this article particularly about dreams. Was purpose mentioned in the "dream" news article or magazine? Write a reflection of your findings and share with the class.

**Log It!**

⚐ Using page 7 as a guide in the Introduction, answer the question in a journal entry on the last time you have reflected on your life. Write about your feelings, where you stand in life, what is against you, what is for you, what you love and what you want to change. Be specific as throughout this book you will learn more on reflecting on your life and making it better.

⚐ During the introduction, Joe Johnson touches on the subject of transformation. What does this word mean to you? Have you ever transformed something? Explain in detail in a journal entry.

# HOME CONNECTION

## Pursue Your Purpose             HOMEWORK

🏠 Think about before and after you read the introduction of this book. After looking at the contents of this book and seeing what you will be learning how do you feel? Discuss with a faculty/staff member at the college and a roommate on what you will be learning from this. Talk with them about their dreams and their story of where they are in their life.

🏠 With a roommate, find a movie or T.V. show that speaks of a story of transformation. What happened? Why was there a motivation for transformation? Think about this as you read the book.

🏠 Make a list of things that you want to transform in your life and why. Have a roommate help you add or eliminate ideas. After you create the list have a discussion with a roommate on why you chose what you did.

The *Pursue Your Purpose* I completed was:

_____
_____.

As a result, I plan to:

_____
_____.

Student Signature: _____ Date: _____

*This sheet may be copied for student use.*

# *Pursue Your Purpose, Not Your Dreams*

## Lesson 2

**Lesson Focus:** This lesson will have students apply their understanding between the differences in defining dreams and defining personal purpose.

**Wise Words:**

| Distinctions | Regrets |
|---|---|
| Destined | Misinterpretations |
| jeopardized | Devastating |
| burnout | Ingrained |
| gratification | Pursue |

**Wise Words Practice:** Choose an activity from the menu on page 7 to introduce words to students in class. Independent student vocabulary practice activities can also be found in corresponding Pathway Portfolio chapter.

**Discuss It:**

⚑ At the beginning of chapter 1 we are introduced to a quote on page 11. Take a few minutes and think what this quote means to you. Share with a partner your thoughts. Then, discuss with the class and apply a real-life example of this quote.

⚑ In chapter one on page 18, Joe Johnson provides a table of values. He explains how values are important to how we live. Take a moment to review the list of values and share with your partner how each value can impact your life in a positive way. Share with the class for further discussion.

**Inscribe It:**

🚩 Joe Johnson describes purpose as, "the reason in which you exist." On pages 15-19 he exclaims "When you find your purpose, you never work a day in your life". What does this mean to you? Explain on a sheet of paper. Make sure to use vivid details in your answer.

🚩 There is a purpose for you and there are your dreams. In chapter one Joe Johnson explains, compares and contrasts both. Create a list of your dreams why are these dreams? Do you think your dream/s are the same as your purpose? Do you think your dreams help you discover your purpose? Explain in a paragraph below your list of dreams.

**Action!:**

🚩 Most of us have dreams for the future. Some dreams come true, but others begin that journey toward their purpose earlier than others. From this day create a 10 year timeline of events that support the dreams you'd like to achieve. Remember, "A dream is something that may or may not come true, but your purpose is *destined* to happen." Get creative to develop your timeline. Be sure to include events. Use color to help enhance your timeline.

🚩 In chapter one Joe Johnson explains that, "When our thoughts and actions have nothing to do with one another and the people around us see something different than what we see in ourselves, we should always reflect and ask ourselves if we're living a dream or our purpose". Create a tri-fold using paper. In the center of the trifold title it BOTH, on the top left of the trifold title it DREAMS, and finally, in the top right of the trifold title it PURPOSE. You may design the outside of your trifold as your choice. On the inside consider the following: Think of your future and what you want to do in life. If money was not an option, what do you think your dreams would be? What do you think your purpose would be? Create at least ten concepts. Once you are finished, consider the "BOTH" section of the trifold, and ask yourself if there are any purposes and dreams that you listed? If so, write them in the center.

🚩 Joe Johnson explains that "Dreams are the perfect example of how sprinting through life could cause us to miss out what is meant for us".

Discuss with a partner possible scenarios for what this means. Include a story line and characters that display what he means. Complete with a partner and share with the class.

**Pursue Possibilities:**

🚩 Research a song or poem that talks about one's purpose or dreams. Analyze the lyrics for a deeper understanding of what this means. How did the artist express this? Write the name and the song lyrics, as well as the artist. For fun, find this song and play it for the class. Get permission from your instructor prior.

🚩 Find an article online, magazine, or news article that speaks of purpose or dreams. You can find a hard copy or online version. Cut or print the article and write a summary on the article and how it relates to the book. Share with a partner or the class. **Log It!**

🚩 In the book on page 12, Joe Johnson speaks of "Mental Decapitation" he refers to this as being " A major experience that makes you change the way you think about something." In a journal entry or video entry describe a time in which you have experienced "mental decapitation". How did this lead you to a new way of thinking? Explain.

🚩 In this chapter the author focuses on defining Dreams and Purpose. Think of yourself in ten years. Write a journal or create a video entry as if you were ten years older. Are you continuing a journey toward one of your Dreams or are you on a journey toward your Purpose? Be descriptive in your entry.

# HOME CONNECTION

## Pursue Your Purpose          HOMEWORK

🏠 Interview a faculty/staff member using questions below about their dreams.

1. What were your dreams when you were younger?
2. Why did you think that was your dream/s?
3. Who or what helped you to have these dreams?
4. Are you living out one of your dreams? Why/Why not?
5. Is what you dreamed of, your Purpose?
6. Tell me your thoughts on Dreams vs. Purpose.

Make notes and have a discussion in comparison to their thoughts. Make notes and have a discussion in comparison to their thoughts.

🏠 With a roommate or friend you are close with, research a TV Show or Movie that displays a character finding their dreams or purpose in life. What was the main idea of the movie or TV Show? Think about the characters involved, how did they take part in finding their purpose or following their dreams? Compare the TV Show or movie to what you have read in chapter one. Discuss with an adult you are close with (preferably a parent or guardian) the similarities or differences.

🏠 Make a trip to a local bookstore or library with a roommate or friend you are close with. Research and find other books focusing on dreams or purpose. After looking at the title page and book summary, compare and discuss with your roommate or friend what you have learned in chapter one.

The *Pursue Your Purpose* I completed was
_____
_____.

As a result, I plan to:
_____
_____.

Student Signature: _____Date: _____

*This sheet may be copied for student use.*

# *Pursue Your Purpose, Not Your Dreams*

## Lesson 3

**Lesson Focus:** This lesson will focus on how family, friends and society impacts the idea of what "cool" really means.

**Wise Words:**

| Professional | Portrayal |
|---|---|
| Influence | Perceptions |
| Internally | Evaluate |
| Coolness | Redefine |
| Befriend | Motivational |

**Wise Words Practice:** Choose an activity from the menu on page 7 to introduce words to students in class.

**Discuss It:**

➤ Think of what it means to be "cool". Take 5 minutes to think of things that make you cool or feel cool. Now, share with your partner. Did you have any similarities in "cool" differences? After a discussion with your partner, share with the class for a further in depth discussion.

➤ In the book on page 24, Joe Johnson provides a list of what could be considered "cool" in our daily lives. Some of these things include hair, skin, teeth and fingernails. Think of these examples and how they are cool. What makes them cool? Who decides it? Share these ideas in detail with the class. Discuss how the media's portrayal of things impacts what becomes cool through citing examples of this.

➤ In chapter 2, we learn that society is teaching us what is cool and what is not. Our family and friends also have been known to influence what is "cool". How do you think this is happening? In what ways have you been influenced by the media? In what ways have you been influenced by your family? Why do you think some people follow what is "cool" and some do not? Think about this and then share with your partner. What ideas did you share? After your discussion with your partner, share with the class.

**Inscribe It:**

⇱ In the chapter, "What is Your Cool?" Joe Johnson discusses the types of people that are cool based on their lifestyle and characteristics. Make a list of people that you think are cool just based on their lifestyle and their external characteristics. Do you think these people would still be cool after you got to know them better? Explain why or why not. After you have written these down, turn to your partner and share your list. Compare and contrast the types of people you discussed, what their lifestyles are and the characteristics that make them seem cool.

⇱ Think about the perception of cool and how it may affect the decisions you make. Think of a time when your decision to do or not to do something was influenced by your desire to be cool. Think of the possible negative and positive consequences of this decision. Create a video reflection or write this in a paragraph and share with the class for further discussion.

**Action!:**

⇱ Using page 24, create a board game using the areas that most people think about being cool. Create cards and game pieces to represent how society creates certain things to be considered cool. In your game, explain for each area why it is cool. For example, "Job", what is a cool job? Why?

⇱ Create a list of what is cool and what isn't cool using the information on page 24. Look at the "what isn't cool" column. What makes these things not cool? What is the deciding factor? Who is the judge and why? Think about your reading on pages 26-27. Apply what you have learned when answering the list.

⇱ Interview students as if you were a news reporter. In this report you must discuss what is cool or not cool, along with the negative and positive consequences related to exhibiting each. Create 10 interview questions involving this concept. Act it out and show how society creates the definition of cool and how you can re-define this. Record your interviews to share with the class.

**Pursue Possibilities:**

🪧 Think about what "cool" has been throughout history. Research what was cool in America throughout the last 115 years. Record and illustrate your findings on a paper or digital timeline. Share it with your class. Research a song or poem that repeats the word cool. What is it about? What can you interpret from this song or poem? Print out a copy of the lyrics or the poem. Share with the class and say the lines out loud. Study the meaning of the song and how the writer or artist used the word cool in context. Create a piece of artwork to illustrate the meaning of cool in the song poem, or any artistic way that fits you.

🪧 Research and create a list of jobs/careers society says are cool. Then make a list of jobs/careers you think are cool. Compare and contrast your lists. Create a media collage of your own cool jobs.

**Log It!**

🪧 Write a journal entry as if you were "society" speaking to the other people who are not cool. In your position as "society", use what you have learned from this chapter on how society, friends and family shape who you are in negative and positive ways. Half the class will take the "negative" stance and the other half will take the "positive" stance. The class will debate after the entries are completed.

🪧 In your journal, create two new beliefs about what is "cool" and sell them to society. With each belief, explain why it is cool. You can use page 24 from the book to help guide your ideas. Share your beliefs with the class. For fun, vote on the best new "cool" belief from the entire class and post them on social media.

🪧 Think about the influence "cool" has on your goals. Consider several examples of this in your own life and write about your thoughts on this in your journal. Consider why it is important to understand the difference between what society "says" you should desire and what is actually best for you.

## HOME CONNECTION

### Pursue Your Purpose          HOMEWORK

🏠 Interview a parent /guardian or an adult close to you when you were younger regarding what they believe is "cool." Be sure to ask how their beliefs impacted the way they guided you when you were younger. Compare your current beliefs of "cool" to their past beliefs of "cool."

🏠 With a roommate or friend, create a contract that allows everyone who signs it to not follow the negative consequences of following society's definition of "cool". Make a promise and hang somewhere that everyone can see each day. In your contract be sure to include the ideas from page twenty four in your book.

🏠 Over time, things that are "cool" have changed. Interview a parent or guardian that recognizes what was "cool" when they were your age. Have them retell you the decades and what and when was cool. Think about what is cool now compared to their times and what they have told you. Discuss why these things change and how society influences this.

The *Pursue Your Purpose* I completed was:
_____
_____.

As a result, I plan to:
_____
_____.


Student Signature: _____ Date: _____

*This sheet may be copied for student use.*

# *Pursue Your Purpose, Not Your Dreams*

## Lesson 4

**Lesson Focus:** In this lesson, students will focus on the meaning of a negative mind and how to live life with positive thinking. Students will be able to demonstrate the impact of living life without focusing on the negative.

**Wise Words:**

| pessimist | Obstacle |
|---|---|
| destructive | Impediment |
| Fixed mindset | Courage |
| barrier | Tenacity |
| Hurdle | Repel |

**Wise Words Practice:** Choose an activity from the menu on page 7 to introduce words to students in class. Independent student vocabulary practice activities can also be found in corresponding Pathways Portfolio chapter.

**Discuss It:**

🚩 Why do you think the author chose not to write about negative thinking in Chapter 3?

🚩 There may have been times that you did not feel your best. Maybe you were sick, tired or lethargic. In these times, you may have complained about the way you felt, or maybe treated someone negatively, or had a different outlook. How did negativity create your thoughts to travel differently in your mind? Why do you think this happens? Identify people in your life that you believe thinks negatively. What is it about them that makes you believe they think negatively? What are some experiences in your life that caused you to think negatively? Think of a specific time where you felt this way. Share with a partner and discuss.

🚩    What do you think the saying, "Focus more on the good and not the bad" means? Do you think you have ever used this thought in a personal situation? How do you think this helps? Would this work in all situations that were negative? Discuss with a partner and share with the class for further discussion.

🚩    Erasing negative thinking can sometimes be a tough obstacle. Think about Thomas Edison for example, it took him 10,000 negative thoughts (failures) to create and invent his light bulb. What if he continued to think negatively? Do you think he would have ever achieved what he did? What do you think kept him moving forward? Think about this and brainstorm times where you could have thought negatively, instead of in a positive way. How would this have changed your outcome? Specifically think about experiences between your senior year in high school up to the present day. Share with a partner and discuss with the class for an in depth understanding.

**Inscribe It:**

🚩    Imagine you are a journalist. Create an advice column or video blog for those people that think negatively. Include a scenario and helpful tips for those to think more positively. You may either make a list (Step 1, Step 2, etc) or write a news article when giving your advice.

🚩    Write a letter to your future self to help remind you to always think and act positively. You may imagine yourself in five years or even more. Give yourself ideas, tips and scenarios that you may be going through in the future. Use experiences that you have been through to help shape your letter.

**Action!:**

🚩    Acknowledge and trash your negative thoughts! On your own or with a partner, create a list of negative thoughts. Write these on small pieces of paper. When finished. Read them out loud to each other and explain why you want to get rid of or trash these negative thoughts. For fun and with an instructor's permission, crumble up the small pieces of paper and throw them in the trash so you can think more positively!

🚩 Write a two-character vignette/scenario that displays a situation exploring one character with negative thoughts and another helping them encouraging positive thinking. Be creative. Share with the class.

🚩 Using multimedia or presentation software, create a skit involving 2 or more characters experiencing negative thinking. In this skit, also include a character, maybe even introduced as yourself. Allow this character to give ideas or advice to other characters that may be thinking in a negative way.

**Pursue Possibilities:**

🚩 Research the definitions and meanings of this lesson's Wise Words. Take all 10 words and create a story. Use several sheets of paper to create a book for fun. Make sure to use all words, and if necessary words may be repeated. Make sure to express the impact of thinking negatively.

🚩 Research a movie or TV show that represents a character who makes a change from thinking negatively to thinking positively. When analyzing the movie or TV show, be sure to take notes about what the character does and how the character's personality changes throughout. Talk about your findings with a partner or the class. Continue to think of the character's thoughts, feelings and emotions and how they grew into positive thinking.

🚩 Positive thinking benefits people in all aspects of their lives. Research a career of your choice. Examine information about the career, interview someone who does this career for a living, and determine how positive thinking has impacted them in their career. Create a 3 slide presentation to give to the class about your findings.

**Log It!**

✝ There may be times where it is hard for you to be positive in difficult, complex situations. In a journal entry, act as if you are the person helping out someone that is thinking negatively. Make sure to apply your understanding on how sometimes it may be difficult to help others think positively. You can use a real-life scenario that you have experienced or, create your own.

✝ Think of a time where it was almost impossible to think positively. In a journal entry or video blog, express what you went through and why it was difficult. Write what you could have done to create more positive thinking. Do you think this would have made the situation better?

## HOME CONNECTION

### Pursue Your Purpose          HOMEWORK

🏠 With a roommate or friend find an old box or shoe box. Use paper to cover the original box. Write on the box **Negative Thoughts.** Make a small opening at the top of the closed box, then, cut small slips of paper that will fit inside the opening. Leave the slips of paper and a writing utensil next to the box somewhere in your home. Have your roommates and friends write their negative thoughts in a box. On one side, write back to them how they can be more positive. Create a routine to use this on a weekly basis with your roommates and friends.

🏠 With a roommate or friend, research and find songs that display negative and positive feelings. What does this artist express in their song to display negative thinking? What does this artist display that shows positive thinking? Compare and contrast several songs. Have a discussion with your roommates or friends on your findings. What are some ways you could help influence the artist to have positive thoughts?

🏠 With the help of a roommate or friend, write a poem that explains a time where you had negative thoughts, but how you have overcame this and changed you're thinking to be positive. Ask your roommate or friend for help on improving negative thinking by asking them for ideas and advice. Have a discussion based on creating positive thinking.

The *Pursue Your Purpose* I completed was:
_____
_____.

As a result, I plan to:
_____
_____.


Student Signature: _____ Date: _____

*This sheet may be copied for student use.*

# *Pursue Your Purpose, Not Your Dreams*

### Lesson 5

**Lesson Focus:** In this lesson, students will be able to understand how stressful situations in life can be impacted and changed with positive thinking. Students will recognize how to get through a rough time in their lives and use positive thoughts.

**Wise Words:**

| Unforeseen | Paralyze |
|---|---|
| Capability | Perceived |
| Commitment | Fortunate |
| Dysfunctional | Rational |
| Internal | Jeopardized |

**Wise Words Practice:** Choose an activity from the menu on page 7 to introduce words to students in class. Independent student vocabulary practice activities can also be found in corresponding Pathways Portfolio chapter.

**Discuss It:**

✝ Think of a time when you were involved in a negative situation during college and remained positive. Was this hard? Why do you think this helped you or even hurt you in the process? What would have changed if you thought differently? Use page thirty five in the book to help guide you when answering this question. Share your thoughts with a partner and the class.

✝ Joe Johnson explained a story about a student he once had a conversation with on thinking more positively. In his conversation, and on page thirty six, think about what he told this specific student. How did this the students improve their positive thinking? Express with a partner and share your thoughts.

✝ In the book on page thirty seven, Joe Johnson poses the question, "Why am I here?" Think about this question and the section written on page thirty seven. Discuss what this means to you and think about what Joe Johnson explains. Express with a partner and then share with the class on your response to this question.

**Inscribe It:**

➤ Think about how you usually feel in college when you are in a "bad mood". How does this affect your actions? How do you affect the people around you? What kind of influences can come about when you are in a bad mood? Give examples of times you have been in a bad mood and why there was a cause for negative thinking. Write a brief reflection and share with your partner.

➤ There are many people that can impact our lives and create negative thinking. On the other hand, there are also people in our lives that have impacted us in a positive way. Create a list of at least 5 people that have impacted you to think more positive or act more positive. On this list describe how and why these people impact you. Share with the class.

**Action!:**

➤ The way we think controls the way we live. Create a brochure on living a positive life. Market your "positive life" using real life scenarios, powerful positive words and testimonials from others that have been using positive thinking in their everyday life. Be creative and use color when designing your brochure. Share with the class.

➤ Make a list of positive things in your life. Be sure to include health, shelter, and living. Now, also create a list of negative things in your life. Create a class poster of everyone's positive and negative things. Have a discussion on how our positives in life outweigh the negatives.

➤ Write down 4-7 negative thoughts that you may face trying to figure out your purpose in life. For example, "I don't thing I like anything." After everyone in the class has finished, trade with a partner or other people in the class. Have several students share the negative thoughts and have a discussion on how to turn this into positive thoughts.

**Pursue Possibilities:**

🚩 Using the internet, research a famous person or athlete that has influenced you to think positively. Create a biography board and a timeline of their life. Include what he/she has contributed to thinking positively and how he/she has influenced other people to be more positive in life. Present this to the class and prepare for discussion on your famous person or athlete.

🚩 Create a 5-10 frame slideshow using presentation software on your research of depression. When you are researching, think about what you have learned from Joe Johnson's book. How does negative thinking link to depression? How does positive thinking help? Be sure to use credible websites and books for your research. Present your findings to the class.

**Log It!**

🚩 Write a journal entry as if you were the student in the story within Chapter 4. What are your responses to what Joe Johnson advises to you? What are your thoughts? What specifically would you respond to from his advice and why? Explain in detail. Share with a partner

🚩 Write a promising journal entry to yourself about thinking positively. Make sure to explain how and why you should do so. Use what you learned in Chapter 4. In your promises, make sure to be specific and use details examples from the text.

## HOME CONNECTION

### Pursue Your Purpose        HOMEWORK

🏠 Create 10 interview questions that you can apply to life scenarios and interview your parent or guardian or a faculty/staff member at your institution. As they respond make sure you ask in detail the when, why and how they stayed positive in negative situations.

🏠 Make a promise phrase with your roommates or friends that you can repeat in any negative situations. Have each of your roommates or friends promise to use this whenever it may apply. For example, "Tough times don't last, but tough people do." Post the phrase somewhere everyone may see.

🏠 Research and find a movie with your roommates or friends that displays a character overcoming a negative situation. How did this character react to their negative situation? What did they do? How did this help them overcome their negative thoughts? Did anyone help or advise them? Have a discussion with your roommates or friends about this movie and the specific character(s).

The *Pursue Your Purpose* I completed was:

_____

_____.

As a result, I plan to:

_____

_____.

Student Signature: _____ Date: _____

*This sheet may be copied for student use*

# *Pursue Your Purpose, Not Your Dreams*

## Lesson 6

**Lesson Focus:** This lesson will focus on how failures and pressure can impact your life. Students will be able to understand how these can help you grow and fulfill the outcomes in your life.

**Wise Words:**

| acknowledge | Considered |
|---|---|
| potential | Dimensional |
| potential | Satisfaction |
| reputation | Anxious |
| pressure | Conquering |

**Wise Words Practice:** Choose an activity from the menu on page 7 to introduce words to students in class. Independent student vocabulary practice activities can also be found in corresponding Pathways Portfolio chapter.

**Discuss It:**

⚐ Do you worry more about others than yourself? How does this affect you? If you focused more on your own well-being, do you think things would change? Discuss with a partner and share your ideas with the class.

⚐ Think about a time in the past when you felt pressured. What was making you feel pressured? Were there any specific people or motivations that created the pressure? Did the situation ease? If so, think about the process and the amount of time that it took. Discuss your story with a partner, share ideas then share with the class.

🚩 Define the word "Failure" in your own words. Think of a time when you experienced failure and what it meant it to you. Take notes and discuss this with your partner. Have students share as a class. Create a list of "failure" definitions from the class and write them on the board or a large white piece of paper. Compare and contrast everyone's diverse definitions.

### Inscribe It:

🚩 How do failures help with success? Think about a time where you have failed but it led you to success. What were the steps that you took to succeed? How did you feel? Create a "How to Overcome Failure" Guide by outlining and explaining each step.

🚩 Think about the positives and negatives of pressure. In small groups, on a large piece of poster board, create a collage of pictures and words showing the positives of pressure on one side and the negatives of pressure on the other side. When you are finished, share with the class. Make sure you share why you chose the pictures or words.

### Action!

🚩 There are many areas in which we may feel a lack of success. Using page fifty four, recognize each area that is listed. Create a scenario for each area based off experiences in your life. You may complete this with a partner if you'd like. Think about the aspects in the situation that could lead to you feeling a lack of success. Create a skit or a video of your scenario and share it with the class.

🚩 There are many famous people in the world who have failed before they have succeeded. For example, a famous person that you may be familiar with, Bill Gates, failed before he become one of the most successful people in the United States. On page fifty five, Joe Johnson compares and explains how he did so. Think of someone with a success story and reflect in your journal why their story stands out to you?

🚩 In our lives, we will encounter many pressures that help us succeed. At home or even with friends we may feel pressure that helps us. Create a skit with your partner that involves a home and school and where pressure may affect you. Make sure to include examples of how it could help you and briefly acknowledge how it could hurt you in life.

**Pursue Possibilities:**

🚩 We've learned of several famous and successful people who have gone through a failure to reach their success. Research a famous person or athlete who has a success story like Jimmy Butler.. Use a multimedia software or presentation software to represent your findings. Make sure to include their biography and life timeline. Share with the class.

🚩 Using your campus, find a random individual that is willing to discuss what it means to fail. Compare that person's experiences to what you have learned. Share your findings with your class.

**Log It!**

🚩 Using page fifty four and the list of areas where you may feel a lack of success, think of the areas that you can agree with for yourself. Which areas are they and why? Be specific. Write in a paragraph form explaining the areas you recognize in yourself and why. Share with the class.

🚩 What if we did not have pressure in our lives? How would this change the way we live our lives? How would this affect our futures? In a journal entry, explain both sides of how pressure would change your life, if you felt it and if you did not feel it. Would this affect your motivation? How would this change your outcomes in life? Explain in detail. Share with a partner.

# HOME CONNECTION

## Pursue Your Purpose     **HOMEWORK**

🏠 Think of what it means to have a "competitive spirit". What does this mean in your family? Interview a parent/guardian or sibling and determine how this looked in your family? How did this relate to pressures in life? Is this a positive or negative thing? Keep notes on what stands out for you.

🏠 Some people say that more negativity, like "pressure", could lead to failure. Talk with a roommate/friend and or parent/guardian on how this could be possible. What type of negativity do you think would cause failure? What kind of negativity could cause success? Discuss with a roommate/friend and or parent/guardian the possible outcomes.

🏠 Together as a class, we will create a promise chart that allows you to have a plan when failures enter your life. Think of failure-type scenarios and how you will handle them. Interview 1-3 individuals on campus or in your family about ways to overcome failures. Be ready to share in small groups and with the class to help formulate a promise chart. Apply what you have learned from this chapter.

The *Pursue Your Purpose* I completed was:
_____
_____.

As a result, I plan to:
_____
_____.


Student Signature: _____ Date: _____

*This sheet may be copied for student use*

# *Pursue Your Purpose, Not Your Dreams*

## Lesson 7

**Lesson Focus:** In this lesson, students will understand how the people you surround yourself with impact your habits and who you become over time. Students will recognize the importance of surrounding themselves with positive individuals who helps them continue to be better. **Wise Words:**

| Maximizing | Potential |
|---|---|
| Destruction | Reputation |
| Recognize | Distinct |
| Unfulfilled | Perspective |
| Identity | Situational |

**Wise Words Practice:** Choose an activity from the menu on page 7 to introduce words to students in class. Independent student vocabulary practice activities can also be found in corresponding Pathways Portfolio chapter.

**Discuss It:**

✝ The people we surround ourselves with influences our habits. If we want to begin or continue on our path of purpose, there may be some things we need to change in our environments, such as the people we surround ourselves with. Explain an idea or scenario that may represent this in your life. Act it out for fun! Be sure to show both negative and positive habits that people may influence you.

✝ On page sixty two, Joe Johnson explains that, "there are so many people who have lived unfilled lives because of situations that caused them to miss out on opportunities". What does this mean? Give specific examples of individuals that have lived or you think are living unfulfilled lives then back is up with "Why." Can you apply this in your life? Explain and share your thoughts with a partner.

🚩 Throughout pages sixty-one through sixty-two, we learn about "checking" ourselves. Think about how this concept relates to you. How are you already checking yourself on a daily basis? What do you accomplish in doing this? Share with a partner, then with a class, by creating a board list of how person checks himself.

**Inscribe It:**

🚩 Create a list of 10 things that you want to do to increase "checking yourself". Be prepared to explain why you hope to increase these things.

🚩 Write a letter or create a video to yourself about your rating of your own self-esteem. How does this relate to checking yourself? Make sure to include points from the text on pages sixty-two through sixty-five. Make sure to include examples, evidence and reasoning.

**Action!**

🚩 Everyone experiences life situations differently, and everyone handles life situations in a different way. Create 5 situations on small index cards, then trade and have a discussion with a small group about how you would react in each situation. Think about each students' response and survey your own response. Learn how everyone reacts and thinks differently. Which situations caused a variety of reactions? Why? Have a post discussion on this topic to further your understanding. Share with the class.

🚩 Identity posters explore who a person is and what they are all about. Create an identity poster for yourself. Think about how identity is described on page sixty-four and how the text explores "distinct characteristics". Create your poster by including your personal values, beliefs and experiences. Use things other than physical characteristics. Be creative with your identity poster. Share your poster with the class and compare and contrast your identifies.

🚩 Create a board game that represents a map. Have the board game involve ideas of identity, values, beliefs and experiences that relate to you. Use stopping points that add scenarios or ideas for each topic. Make your own game pieces for fun. You may complete this with a partner or on your own. Share your board games to learn more about the other students in your class.

**Pursue Possibilities:**

🚩 To further your research on this chapter, use the internet to explore identity and ideas of values and beliefs from other people in the world. Define what you believe your purpose is in life. Include who you are and your biography that supports your purpose. Create a presentation using multimedia presentation software to represent your findings and discovered purpose.

🚩 Athletes, famous people and self-esteem all come together. We've learned this from what we have been reading in this chapter. Now, create a video and act as a famous person or athlete. Use research from their biography and list in the video what you think their purpose is, what their identity is like, and their values and believes. Make sure to dress and speak like the person you choose to get the full effect! You can represent your findings in your video and present to the class.

**Log It!**

🚩 Write a journal or video reflection about your self-esteem prior to reading this chapter and now after reading this chapter. Compare and contrast your emotions and feelings on this subject and what you have learned. How can self-esteem affect who you are and the decisions that you make that help you live your life? Explain in detail.

🚩 Express in writing in a journal entry format using pages sixty-five through page sixty-eight. Think of yourself as an athlete and how your self-esteem helped you get where you are. How can your self-esteem affect your life? Be specific. Use examples from the text to support your writing.

## HOME CONNECTION

**Pursue Your Purpose**          **HOMEWORK**

🏠 There are many words that represent self-esteem and the effects of self-esteem in our life. Create a list with a roommate/friend or parent/guardian that explores positive and negative words involving the self-esteem. Leave this list somewhere for everyone to see. Make a point to use the positive words on a daily basis to keep positive effects on your self-esteem.

🏠 Many famous people have written quotes for motivational purposes. Now that you have learned about the effects of self-esteem, create your own quote to help others continue to have positive impacts on self-esteem. Have a roommate/friend or a parent/guardian help you create this. Make a large drawing of this to hang somewhere close to you.

🏠 Discuss with your parent/guardian or close family member the differences between physical characteristics and emotions, beliefs, and values. How can these different aspects of your identity cause misconceptions? Create a chart comparing and contrasting these. You can use a computer program or a sheet of paper to represent the differences. Use and apply what you learned from this chapter on identity.

The *Pursue Your Purpose* I completed was:
_____
_____ .

As a result, I plan to:
_____
_____ .

Student Signature: _____ Date: _____

*This sheet may be copied for student use.*

# *Pursue Your Purpose, Not Your Dreams*

## Lesson 8

**Lesson Focus:** In this lesson, students will focus on the concept of rebuilding. This lesson helps students understand that everyone may experience a time in their life that may require rebuilding and steps they can take to enrich the process for better outcomes.

**Wise Words:**

| Rebuilding | Exposing |
|---|---|
| Dismantle | Academically |
| transitioning | Committing |
| engaged | Attempted |
| reassemble | Outcome |

**Wise Words Practice:** Choose an activity from the menu on page 7 to introduce words to students in class. Independent student vocabulary practice activities can also be found in corresponding Pathways Portfolio chapter.

**Discuss It:**

✝ On page seventy-three in the text, Joe Johnson explains that everyone experiences some type of rebuilding process in their life. Think of a time where you may have done this. Why and what did you accomplish in this rebuilding time? Share with a partner to compare experiences. Come together as a class for further discussion on this topic.

✝ Think of the words: repair, dismantle and reassemble. What do these three words mean to you? Describe or define these in your own words. Look at page seventy-four in the text for assistance. Compare and contrast the meaning of these three.

🚩 Fear. On page seventy-six Joe Johnson explains FEAR as an acronym, "Forget Everything and Run" and "Finding Excused About Reality". Why are these acronyms negative concepts to have? When defining fear how does this affect the outcome? Does it make it worse or better? Discuss your thoughts with a partner.

**Inscribe It:**

🚩 Writing your goals down can help you realize what you want to accomplish in your life, and even when you want to accomplish them. During a rebuilding process in your life, setting a timeline (when) is also important. You must think of where you are, at the time of the rebuilding process and where you need or want to be in a certain amount of time. Create a list of end goals that you think will or would help you in a rebuilding process. Keep in mind you are in college and what you do during this time impacts your future goals.

🚩 You must be comfortable not knowing the outcome of your rebuilding process. Why do you think this is important to do? How would knowing the outcome affect your strength and how would knowing the outcome affect the entirety of your rebuilding process. Write in your journal or create a video blog on your thoughts. Share with a partner or the class for further discussion.

**Action!:**

🚩 Understanding the rebuilding process and the steps it may take is important in applying it to a real life situation. Create an advice column, like you would find in a newspaper. In this, make sure to include the entry letter of a college student that is having a problem picking a major and needs to rebuild. In your response, use advice and apply what you have learned in this chapter. You can write it or type it.

✝ Using the vocabulary words from this chapter that are listed at the beginning of the lesson, create a list of your top three words and prepare an introduction using these words. This introduction of the words can only be 30 seconds and the introduction should help individuals understand why these words mean so much to you. Be creative.

✝ Act it out! With a partner, or a group, create a skit that represents a possible rebuilding process during college. Make sure to have someone in your group direct the person who is rebuilding with positive advice. Be creative in your skit. Present to the class for fun.

**Pursue Possibilities:**

✝ Using the internet or a book as a resource, research stories about people overcoming fear. What did you find? Make a list of resources and information that you found. Bring to class and share with your partners and the class. What did you find together as a group?

✝ Research a song that speaks or talks about fear. What are the lyrics? What do they mean to you? How do they apply to fear? What is the artist relaying about fear? Do you think there was a motivation behind this song? Could you give them any advice that you learned in this chapter? Write down your thoughts and share with a partner and or the class.

**Log It!**

✝ Using page seventy-nine in the text, write a journal entry on how fear has interfered with a process in your life. Think about your childhood all the way to the present day. Make sure to include details on this time in your life. Where did it come from? How did it impact you then and now? Were there individuals that fueled your fear in a negative way?

✝ Prepare for a battle of fear. Using page seventy-eight in the text, think of how you will react to "fear" in the future. Pretend you are in your senior year of college. Create a journal or video blog entry as if you have something to fear. What is it? Why are you having fear against this? How do you stand up against it? Be descriptive. Using page seventy-nine in the text, discuss how fear has interfered with a process in your life. Make sure to include details on this time in your life.

## HOME CONNECTION

### Pursue Your Purpose        HOMEWORK

🏠 Interview a parent/guardian or close family member on a time they had to rebuild or dismantle a time in their life. What was their experience? How does this connect to Joe Johnson's experience in this chapter? Have a discussion with a parent/guardian or close family member and compare and contrast the two situations. Think about the variables such as age, time and lifestyle when discussing.

🏠 Create a plan with your roommates, friends, or family that will include the steps you will follow if you experience a time to dismantle, reassemble or rebuild your life. Make sure to include your attitude and ideas during the rebuilding process.

🏠 Find a puzzle or something to rebuild in real life. Have a parent/guardian, close family friend or roommate halo you. How was this process? How can you compare this to a real life rebuilding process that you may experience? How is this similar and how can this be different. Have a discussion while you are completing this activity.

The *Pursue Your Purpose* I completed was:
_____
_____.

As a result, I plan to:
_____
_____.

Student Signature: _____ Date: _____

*This sheet may be copied for student use.*

# *Pursue Your Purpose, Not Your Dreams*

## Lesson 9

**Lesson Focus:** In this lesson students will recognize the many ISM's of life. Students will be able to understand the negative impact that these ISM's hold and how to overcome and or understand the impact they hold.

**Wise Words:**

| Heterosexism | Superiority |
|---|---|
| Interactions | Covert |
| Ableism | Overt |
| Capacities | Microagressions |
| Sexism | Classism |
| Racism | Homophobia |

**Wise Words Practice:** Choose an activity from the menu on page 7 to introduce words to students in class. Independent student vocabulary practice activities can also be found in corresponding Pathways Portfolio chapter.

**Discuss It:**

⌖ We all see the world through a different lenses based on our experiences. Look at page eighty-two, how does this apply to you? Do you agree? Why or why not? Think about what this means and be prepared to share with a partner or the class.

⌖ ISM's are important because of the way they impact our interactions and the way that we view others. What do they mean to you? Explain in your own words. Compare and contrast your thoughts with a partner.

⌖ Using page eighty-three in the text, look at the table that is listed. Think of the ISM's that we already know. Which ones are they? How did you originally learn about these? Explain and share and compare with your partner. Did you share the same ones, or different. Then, share with the class on what you came up with.

**Inscribe It:**

🚩 Using the quote on page eighty-two, "We all see the world through a certain lens that is shaped by our experiences" Write in a paragraph form what you think the author means by this. Can you relate to what they are saying? Be vivid in explaining in detail. If possible, use a scenario to support your writing.

🚩 This chapter is about the ISM's in life that we may experience. From what you have read and what you have witnessed in your own life, what ISM's have you seen the most? Why? Share and compare your writing with a partner.

**Action!:**

🚩 ISM's are important to understand because they impact our life. Make a board of your choice with 8 columns. Label each of these ISM's you learned about a describe possible situations where they could take place. When you are finished, share with the class.

🚩 Using the vocabulary words provided, and other words that relate to the ISM's of this chapter, create a set of interview questions centered around three of the ISM's that have impacted individuals in the group. Each group consists of three members. Each member should create two to four open ended questions each. Be ready to share questions in class.

🚩 Using the interview questions your group created, go on campus and interview PEOPLE YOU DO NOT KNOW. Pay attention to how many are willing to answer, gauge how comfortable individuals seem to be, and ask if they are willing to answer the questions on video.

🚩 Using the ISM's in this chapter, have a charade contest with the class. Divide the class into teams or into two groups. Have the ISM's listed on small pieces of paper, Have each team member draw from a hat each ISM. Have them act it out and their team guess which ISM. For fun, the person acting out each ISM may use audience volunteers to act in the charade.

**Pursue Possibilities:**

✝ We have learned that ISM's are important because they impact our interactions. Research a specific ISM and find where this specific ISM impacted someone or something. After your research be prepared to share with the class your findings. Keep a track of your resources and information.

✝ When you understand other factors in your environment it becomes part of a rebuilding process in your life. We may have been taught something different at home or in our childhood, but as we grow and rebuild parts of our life we may experience ISM's. Write about a time where one of the ISM's impacted you. Keep your story between one and two pages. Allow your partner to read your story aloud back to you. Think about what you have learned in this chapter when writing your story.

**Log It!**

✝ Misconceptions are a big issue in ISM's. Write what you think or how they relate to each other. You may complete this as a journal entry or in the form of a list. If you'd like, share with a partner your writing.

✝ Write a journal entry as if you were witnessing an ISM on campus. Discuss how you think you would feel, react, and handle the situation. Make sure to be detailed in your entry.

## HOME CONNECTION

**Pursue Your Purpose**          **HOMEWORK**

🏠 Interview a parent/guardian or someone older than you that has known you since your childhood. Interview them about a time that they have witnessed one of the ISM's you have learned about. What was their experience like? What was the ISM they witnessed? Have a discussion on what you have learned in this chapter and apply to their story.

🏠 Identify one or two faculty/staff members on campus that provide trainings or do research regarding the ISM's. Interview them and ask them to help you come up with ways to identify ISM's within yourself. Be sure to think about what you have learned in this chapter.

🏠 With a roommate or friends, research and find a movie that represents one of the ISM's that were mentioned in this chapter. When watching the movie look and think about the characters and their positions. How were they connected to an ISM? Think about all the factors with this specific character and the main idea of the movie.

The *Pursue Your Purpose* I completed was:
_____
_____.

As a result, I plan to:
_____
_____.


Student Signature: _____ Date: _____

*This sheet may be copied for student use.*

# *Pursue Your Purpose, Not Your Dreams*

## Lesson 10

**Lesson Focus:** In this lesson students learn the importance of being a part of a team. Students will be able to understand and recognize how a team can be positive and allow them to fulfill their life and purpose.

**Wise Words:**

| Inherited | Encouragement |
|-----------|---------------|
| Mindful | Presence |
| Accountable | Sacrificing |
| Progressing | Franchise |
| mastered | Aligned |

**Wise Words Practice:** Choose an activity from the menu on page 7 to introduce words to students in class. Independent student vocabulary practice activities can also be found in corresponding Pathways Portfolio chapter.

**Discuss It:**

✝ Think about what being part of a team means to you. Have you ever played a sport or have been in a group that needed teamwork? Explain your experiences and the importance's you have learned of being a part of a team. Share and compare your experiences with a partner.

✝ Create a list of examples in real life that require teamwork. Think of scenarios where you cannot do things alone. In your list be sure to have details and support. Share your thoughts with the class. Make a class list.

✝ Think about someone who does not enjoy being on a team. Have you ever felt this way? Why do you think they are uninterested in being a part of a team? Discuss with a partner your thoughts and findings.

**Inscribe It:**

🚩 Looking at page one hundred and two as a reference, think about what Joe Johnson says, "How often have you taken the time to think about the type of people you need on your team to win championships in the game of life". What does he mean by "game of life"? How can you respond to this? Have you taken the time to think about the type of people you need? Who are they or what would their character be like? In a paragraph form explain in detail.

🚩 On page one hundred seven, Joe Johnson explains that, "Building our team is vital to our journey toward our purpose". In your own words respond to what he is saying. Give examples or even a real life scenario to support your thoughts. Share your writing with a partner and compare.

**Action!:**

🚩 In this chapter we learn about the 4P's: You are a Product of the People you Place in your Presence. Think about your team (the people closest to you). Make a list of the top 3-7 people on your team. Next ask yourself, "Why are they on your team?" Lastly, ask yourself who should no longer be on your team? Refer to the chapter regard the importance of having a team.

🚩 In small groups, identify a specific field or position to focus on. Create an ideal team that is needed to get you to this field or position and be successful. Be creative when developing the ideal team. Use tools and rules that explore the importance of teamwork.

**Pursue Possibilities:**

🚩 Using the internet or book resources research a famous athlete. In this person's biography or timeline of athletic events, find a writing or quote that they have said about teamwork. How do your findings relate to what we have learned in this chapter? Record your resources and findings on this athlete. Be prepared to share your research with the class.

🚩 There are many sports teams that have been successful in championships, and have often repeated their success. Research a sports team that have done this. Use resources from the internet or books to help you learn more about their journey. Create a presentation using a computer. Use pictures, story clips, and biographies about this sports team. Share and present to the class.

**Log It!**

🚩 Imagine you are a famous CEO of your own company. Write a journal entry as if your company were receiving an award for #1 company in the world.. Write about the importance of having your team come together to accomplish company goals . Be descriptive in detail. Use characters and specific events in your entry. Think about what we have learned in this chapter on the importance of teamwork in the journey to find our purpose in life.

🚩 In a journal entry, write about a time where you have been a part of a team. This could be from a school event or maybe you played on a team of some sort. How did your team help you accomplish or achieve things? Explain using examples to support your writing.

## HOME CONNECTION

**Pursue Your Purpose**          **HOMEWORK**

🏠 Meet with the individuals you listed in the 4P's exercise. Have a discussion with about teamwork. Make sure to ask about their role in helping you move toward your purpose.

🏠 Research and find a movie that involves teamwork, with specifically one character or team. What is the movie's purpose? What were the characters like? Were there any characters that did not want to be a part of a team?

Compare and contrast this movie with what we have learned in this chapter. Have a roommate or friend help you with answer these questions for further discussion.

🏠 Discuss with a parent how your family can be a team in helping you through the journey of finding your purpose. What do they do on a daily basis to support you in your life? How do you support them? How does this help you get to where you want to be in life? Keep in mind the importance of team work and it affects your purpose in life.

The *Pursue Your Purpose* I completed was:
_____
_____.

As a result, I plan to:
_____
_____.


Student Signature: _____ Date: _____

*This sheet may be copied for student use.*

# *Pursue Your Purpose, Not Your Dreams*

## Lesson 11

**Lesson Focus:** In this lesson, students will be able to differentiate between purpose and dreams. Students will be able to apply what they have learned throughout the entire book and apply their understanding of having a purpose and how to follow their dreams.

**Wise Words:**

| Translate | Journey |
|---|---|
| Possibilities | Pressure |
| Conditioned | Interpretation |
| Acceptance | Role |
| Phrases | Passion |

**Wise Words Practice:** Choose an activity from the menu on page 7 to introduce words to students in class. Independent student vocabulary practice activities can also be found in corresponding Pathways Portfolio chapter.

**Discuss It:**

⚑ After reading page one hundred twelve, think about what Joe Johnson says, "Although dreams are something that may or may not come true, dreams are important because it gives us the ability to create the will power to keep moving during times where there may or may not be options." What does this mean to you? Can you relate or explain in your own words what he is saying? When you are finished share and compare with a partner. Did your partner have something similar in mind as you? Explore and further your discussion with the class.

⚑ In the text on page one hundred fourteen Joe Johnson quotes by saying, "No matter where you are from, your dreams are valid". How does this relate to you? What is the difference between the phrases, "Follow your dreams" and "Your dreams are valid?" Have you ever felt undetermined or had a lack of motivation because of where you are from? Think about this statement. How can you change your thoughts? And why is this important to apply in your life. Share with the class when you have your thoughts gathered.

🪧 Everyone will have their own journey, their own dreams and their own purpose. Now is the time to share what your dreams are and how your purpose will take you on your life's journey. Think about your plan and share with a partner. Discuss with your partner on how you will carry out your journey.

**Inscribe It:**

🪧 Your journey sometimes includes both your purpose in life and your dreams. When you think about your "purpose," what makes this difficult to accomplish or even foresee in the future? Is there anything holding you back? Think about this and write down your thoughts in paragraph form. Share with the class for further discussion an investigation on how you can achieve your purpose and dreams without anything holding you back.

🪧 Defining your identity will help you create your journey toward your purpose. However, dreams seem to always find itself into our lives. How do you think your actions will affect each of these (purpose/dreams)? Will these change overnight? Or is this a process? Explain in detail your answer. Use evidence from this chapter to support your writing.

**Action!:**

🪧 Create a list of the steps you will take to begin or continue on your journey toward your purpose. How difficult will it be to use the steps to continue the journey? Use this text to help you review the important aspects in your journey.

🪧 From what you have learned in this chapter and the previous nine chapters, create a "One Pager" summarizing this book. Make sure to include how this book helped you better understand your life's purpose. Make sure to present these "One Pager's" to class as a reminder for everyone to fulfill their purpose in life.

⚑ Create two scenarios that you and a partner can act out. Have one scenario focus on "purpose" and the other scenario focus on "dreams". Make sure that in your scenario you have aspects that easily define and differentiate between the two. You may involve other partners in the class for this activity. Have the class act out each scenario. For fun, guess each other's scenario if they are "dreams" or "purposes".

**Pursue Possibilities:**

⚑ Quotes are important in motivating you for your journey in life. Find three different quotes that you feel will help you and others stay motivated in your journey toward your purpose. Keep track of your resources and the people that have originally said these quotes. If possible further your research on the biographies of these people. Find a movie, film or TV Episode that displays a motivational idea to help you and others on your purpose. Does this movie, film or TV Episode have dreams and purposes with the characters? Analyze the movie, film or TV Episode from what you have learned in this book. Share your thoughts with a partner or the class for further discussion.

**Log It!**

⚑ Imagine yourself five years from now. Write a biography of where you have been, what you have experienced and make sure to note where you are on your journey. Have you fulfilled opportunities? Are you pursuing your purpose? Or are you still pursuing your dreams? Be specific and make sure to also include your age and the people who are in your life at that time.

⚑ Write a letter to a loved one, someone younger than you, who may not understand what a purpose is or what dreams really mean in your life. Give them advice on how to handle their journey using what you have learned from this book. Share your letter with the class and explain your reasoning on writing a letter to this specific person.

# HOME CONNECTION

## Pursue Your Purpose         HOMEWORK

🏠 With your roommates, create a motivational quote that displays dreams and purpose. Hang this somewhere in the home or where everyone can see it. Use what you have learned in this book and make sure to discuss the importance of utilizing each aspect of this book to motivate your journey.

🏠 Discuss with an older family member, such as a grandparent, on what their journey has been like. Take notes and use what you have learned in this book to interview them on if they have had a purpose in their life, and what their dreams were. Make sure to take note of their experiences using a notebook.

🏠 Researching people in the past can help everyone learn on what paths they want to take. Find a person, in the field that you think you want to be in and research their journey. As you research determine if they were pursuing their dreams or purpose and why you believe it. This may be done at your local library or using the internet. Have a roommate or family member help you. Have a discussion on your findings.

The *Pursue Your Purpose* I completed was:
_____
_____.

As a result, I plan to:
_____
_____.

Student Signature: _____ Date: _____

*This sheet may be copied for student use.*

# *Pursue Your Purpose, Not Your Dreams*

**Lesson 12          Wise Words**

**Lesson Focus:** This lesson will have students apply their understanding of the entirety of this book and be able to apply what they learned in reality.

**Wise Words:**

| Possibility | Issues |
|---|---|
| Overshadows | Maturity |
| Purposefully | Guidance |
| Mental | Concerned |
| Circumstances | Syndrome |

**Wise Words Practice:** Choose an activity from the menu on page 7 to introduce words to students in class. Independent student vocabulary practice activities can also be found in corresponding Pathway Portfolio chapter.

**Discuss It:**

✝ In Joe Johnson's "Wise Words" at the end of the book, he starts off the chapter with a story of someone having problems in their college classroom. Have you ever had problems with a teacher or an instructor and you had too much pride to talk about it? Think about your past and share with a partner your feelings. Compare and contrast stories with one another.

✝ Having too much pride may affect you in a negative way. With a partner discuss these possibilities and compare and contrast how in reality this may happen. Share personal experiences and your thoughts with the class.

**Inscribe It:**

🚩 Create a list of the pros and cons to asking questions in college situations where you may feel you have too much pride. What are the positive things and what are the negative things. Who do these affect most? Think about the possibilities when creating your list. Share with a partner or the class for further discussion.

🚩 Joe Johnson exemplifies how asking questions can make us feel weak. How is this possible? Think of a time when you felt this way. Write down your thought process of not wanting to ask the question or even ask for help. If you would like, share your thoughts with partner to compare and contrast your stories.

**Action!:**

🚩 Create an acronym for Pride. Use a large piece of paper to describe each letter. Share with the class the meaning of your acronym.

🚩 Asking more questions in life can lead us to larger thinking and more knowledge. Think about why people do not ask questions when they do not know the answer. As a class, create a game where teams try to guess the answer without asking questions. Each team picks an object in the room and other teams must guess which object they picked without asking questions. For fun, keep track of the amount of time it takes to guess the object. The team with the least amount of time wins.

🚩 This book has helped with information on living your life now, and in the future. Make a short video on this book and sell it! Use what you have learned to market and help others create a better or new way of thinking based on what you learned.

**Pursue Possibilities:**

🚩 Research a movie or T.V. show that depicts a character having to much pride. What were your findings? Were there advantages and disadvantages to this character? How was their life? Apply what you have learned from this book. Give this character advice in a newspaper column to help them understand how to live a better future, or help them transform using "Wise Words."

⚐ Research and look for famous people with that have the same vision as Joe Johnson. Discovering our purpose in life are important. What is their message? Did they write a book? Explain your findings in paragraph form. Share with the class and compare and contrast your findings

**Log It!**

⚐ What were your favorite parts of this book? Did you learn many things that you can apply in your life? What were they? Write down your thoughts in a journal entry.

⚐ After reading this book, we have learned many new tactics that we can apply in our realities. Write a letter to someone explaining what you have learned, why it is important and how they can apply this in their life as you are.

## HOME CONNECTION

**Pursue Your Purpose**           **HOMEWORK**

🏠 Share the content of what you have learned with a roommate or friend. Discuss the items and topics that you have decided to transform in your life and why. Make sure to include how this will positively affect your life and your future family's life.

🏠 Make a trip to the local bookstore and find a similar book that may help with transforming your life with a better vision. Read this book and share your thoughts with a roommate, friend, or family member. Compare and contrast the books' main idea with the one you have read.

🏠 Create a list of reasons to read this book again. Share your thoughts with a roommate, friend, or family member on what you have learned and how this may help others in their future experiences.

The *Pursue Your Purpose* I completed was:
_____
_____.

As a result, I plan to:
_____
_____.


Student Signature: _____ Date: _____

*This sheet may be copied for student use.*

***Pursue Your Purpose, Not Your Dreams***

**Assessments**

# *My Purpose Pathway* Checklist

## *How do I know if I am "pursuing my purpose"?*

**Check all that apply today.**

- ☐ I train for my long distance run by doing things now to prepare myself along the way.
- ☐ I take time to know myself.
- ☐ My actions and values are aligned.
- ☐ I am comfortable with the uncomfortable.
- ☐ I have built a solid team to support me.
- ☐ I think an speak positively.
- ☐ I take steps to overcome fear.
- ☐ I ask for help as needed.
- ☐ I have a clear understanding of "ism's".
- ☐ I have changed to why I think about purpose and dreams.
- ☐ I have moved beyond "cool".
- ☐ I am focused pursuing my purpose rather than society's dreams.

Pairing this checklist of behaviors is a great way to track your own progress in pursuing your purpose! The Purpose Pathway rubric on the next page provides a way for you to measure your progress.

# *Pursue Your Purpose* Rubric:

**Student Name:**
_____

**Date:**
_____

**Daily Goal:**
_____

1 – displayed **very few or no** *Pursue Your Purpose* behaviors today

2 – displayed **a few** *Pursue Your Purpose* behaviors today

3 – displayed **several** *Pursue Your Purpose* behaviors today

4 – displayed **many** *Pursue Your Purpose* behaviors today

*Complete and initial the Self Rating (S). Ask your teacher complete and initial the Teacher Rating (T).*

| Teacher/Period | Monday | Tuesday | Wednesday | Thursday | Friday | Total |
|---|---|---|---|---|---|---|
| Self | 1 2 3 4 | 1 2 3 4 | 1 2 3 4 | 1 2 3 4 | 1 2 3 4 | S = |
| Teacher | 1 2 3 4 | 1 2 3 4 | 1 2 3 4 | 1 2 3 4 | 1 2 3 4 | T = |
| Self | 1 2 3 4 | 1 2 3 4 | 1 2 3 4 | 1 2 3 4 | 1 2 3 4 | S = |
| Teacher | 1 2 3 4 | 1 2 3 4 | 1 2 3 4 | 1 2 3 4 | 1 2 3 4 | T = |
| Self | 1 2 3 4 | 1 2 3 4 | 1 2 3 4 | 1 2 3 4 | 1 2 3 4 | S = |
| Teacher | 1 2 3 4 | 1 2 3 4 | 1 2 3 4 | 1 2 3 4 | 1 2 3 4 | T = |
| Self | 1 2 3 4 | 1 2 3 4 | 1 2 3 4 | 1 2 3 4 | 1 2 3 4 | S = |
| Teacher | 1 2 3 4 | 1 2 3 4 | 1 2 3 4 | 1 2 3 4 | 1 2 3 4 | T = |
| Self | 1 2 3 4 | 1 2 3 4 | 1 2 3 4 | 1 2 3 4 | 1 2 3 4 | S = |
| Teacher | 1 2 3 4 | 1 2 3 4 | 1 2 3 4 | 1 2 3 4 | 1 2 3 4 | T = |
| Self | 1 2 3 4 | 1 2 3 4 | 1 2 3 4 | 1 2 3 4 | 1 2 3 4 | S = |
| Teacher | 1 2 3 4 | 1 2 3 4 | 1 2 3 4 | 1 2 3 4 | 1 2 3 4 | T = |
| Self | 1 2 3 4 | 1 2 3 4 | 1 2 3 4 | 1 2 3 4 | 1 2 3 4 | S = |
| Teacher | 1 2 3 4 | 1 2 3 4 | 1 2 3 4 | 1 2 3 4 | 1 2 3 4 | T = |
| Self | 1 2 3 4 | 1 2 3 4 | 1 2 3 4 | 1 2 3 4 | 1 2 3 4 | S = |
| Teacher | 1 2 3 4 | 1 2 3 4 | 1 2 3 4 | 1 2 3 4 | 1 2 3 4 | T = |
| Self | 1 2 3 4 | 1 2 3 4 | 1 2 3 4 | 1 2 3 4 | 1 2 3 4 | S = |
| Teacher | 1 2 3 4 | 1 2 3 4 | 1 2 3 4 | 1 2 3 4 | 1 2 3 4 | T = |

*\*\*Graph your data to view clearer results!*

**Student Name:**_____

# *Pursue Your Purpose* Pre / Post Test

1. When Joe Johnson refers to, "Mental Decapitation", what does he mean?

    a. When your mentality is chopped off
    b. When you have a major experience that makes you change the way you think about something
    c. When you make distinctions between Purposes and life
    d. When you change the way you do something

2. Dreams are not a _____ of how sprinting through life could cause us to miss out on what is meant for us.

    a. Good example
    b. Good reference
    c. Bad example
    d. Bad connection

3. Dreams are okay to have as long as you are not:
    a. Imagining things that cannot happen
    b. Uncovering surface layers of the world
    c. Go outside of your environment
    d. Sprinting through life

4. Purpose is the reason in which you _____.
    a. Live
    b. Exist
    c. Explore
    d. Engage

5. Three examples of values listed in the book are:
    a. Honesty, Truthfulness, Engagement
    b. Money, Power, Humbleness
    c. Happiness, Trust, Exploration
    d. Education, Leadership, Disrespect

6. What are two areas that are mentioned in the book as that we may think are connected with being "Cool":

    a. Boyfriend, Skateboards
    b. Hygiene, Finances
    c. Animals, Wife
    d. Hair, How we sing

7. Depression is sometimes described as feeling sad, _____, and _____ or down.

    a. Happy, Anxious
    b. Excited, Ambitious
    c. Unhappy, Miserable
    d. Miserable, Pleasant

8. The way we think will control the way we live and the way we live will sometimes control:

    a. How long we live
    b. How we grow
    c. How we can change over time
    d. How we will end

9. The first type of "worrying" is about everyone else, the second type of worrying is about:

    a. The environment
    b. Society
    c. Family, friends or someone we may or may not know is doing
    d. animals

10. Pressure is often defined as:

    a. The action of a force against an opposing force
    b. The stress or urgency of matters demanding attention
    c. The burden of physical or mental distress
    d. All of the above

11. Pressure seems to shift the mind into:
    a. 3D
    b. One dimensional thinking
    c. Time zone changes
    d. Negative outcomes

12. Failure is defined as:

    a. The condition or fact of not achieving the desired end or ends
    b. A lack of success
    c. Doing everything wrong
    d. A and/or B

13. Checking ourselves means:

    a. Recognizing the people we surround ourselves with and the bad habits we may have picked up from years of doing something the same way over and over again.
    b. Changing the way we do things
    c. Hanging around only two or three people
    d. Looking at our clothes before we leave our house

14. Joe Johnson defines Self-Esteem as:

    a. Having bad thoughts about who you are
    b. How you feel about others
    c. The confidence you have in yourself
    d. How other people see you

15. The word, "rebuild" means:

    a. Mix
    b. Spin

c. Repair, Dismantle or Reassemble
d. check

16. Fear makes us believe that:
    a. Everything is impossible
    b. The "something is different for me" is not available
    c. We cannot follow through with what we want
    d. We can't explore our future

17. Two ISM's that are mentioned in this book are:
    a. Sexism, Ageism
    b. Ageism, Timeism
    c. Classism, Technoism
    d. Workism, Sportsism

18. Classism can be defined as:
    a. The set order of classes
    b. Organization of social classes
    c. Prejudice or discrimination based on class
    d. Class action

19. The 4P's are:

    a. Posture, Purpose, Pioneering, Pilot
    b. Product, People, Place, Presence
    c. Pivot, Primary, Punctual, Posture
    d. Polynomial, Prime, Place, People

20. Building our team is vital to our _____ toward our
    _____.

    a. Car, House
    b. Vision, Destination
    c. Mindset, Vision
    d. Journey, purpose


21. The definition of "situation self-esteem" is:

    a. You lack self-esteem
    b. You only have self-esteem at home

  c. You have high self-esteem in one area of life and low self-esteem in other areas
  d. You lack positive thinking

22. Every journey to purpose begins _____.
  a. Someday
  b. Somehow
  c. Some way
  d. Somewhere

23. Two areas in where we may feel a lack of success are:

  a. Home, Gym
  b. Sports, Jobs/Careers
  c. Marriage, Art
  d. Dreams, Siblings

24. "Keep it 100" means:

  a. To tell a lie
  b. To give money
  c. To earn 100 dollars
  d. When someone wants the truth

25. "Keep it Real" means:
  a. To live in realty
  b. To tell something with full truth
  c. To recognize realty
  d. To show who your real friends are

# *Pursue Your Purpose*
# Pre / Post Test Answer Key

1. b
2. a
3. d
4. b
5. c
6. b
7. c
8. a
9. c
10. d
11. b
12. d
13. a
14. c
15. c
16. b
17. a
18. c
19. b
20. d
21. c
22. d
23. b
24. d
25. b

Made in the USA
Middletown, DE
18 February 2024

49498260R00038